S0-BJL-954

POSTCARD HISTORY SERIES

West Point

SCENES FROM WEST POINT. Almost since the first days of the United States Military Academy at West Point, tourists have been attracted to the scenic vistas, unique architecture, historic significance, and dashing young cadets in uniform. A booming tourism industry flourished in the neighboring villages and gift shops offering memorabilia provided visitors with souvenirs. Picture postcards began to be widely circulated in 1898, and views of West Point and cadets became a popular collectible. (Courtesy of Col. [Ret.] Seth Hudgins, USMA 1964.)

On the front cover: **GUARD MOUNT.** At one point in West Point's history, guard mount was one of the most interesting ceremonies in the daily routine at West Point. The cadets would stand at attention in full dress uniform, and a thorough inspection would take place. After inspection, cadets would begin sentry guard or some other duty. Today's cadets prepare periodically for Saturday morning inspection (SAMI). Upperclassmen thoroughly check rooms, closets, beds, and uniforms for violations, and gigs are noted. (Courtesy of Peter E. Carroll.)

On the back cover: **BIRD'S-EYE VIEW, WEST POINT.** In this aerial view of West Point, the Doubleday Field, home of army baseball, comes into view. Named for Abner Doubleday, USMA 1842, the baseball field has expanded and now includes a beautiful stadium. Doubleday is credited with forming the modern game of baseball. There is considerable evidence to refute the claim. (Courtesy of Peter E. Carroll.)

POSTCARD HISTORY SERIES

West Point

Maureen Oehler DuRant and Peter E. Carroll

ARCADIA
PUBLISHING

Published by Arcadia Publishing
Charleston, South Carolina

Printed in the United States of America

Library of Congress Catalog Card Number: 2007927921

For all general information contact Arcadia Publishing at:
Telephone 843-853-2070
Fax 843-853-0044
E-mail sales@arcadiapublishing.com
For customer service and orders:
Toll-Free 1-888-313-2665

Visit us on the Internet at www.arcadiapublishing.com

For my cadet: play hard, work harder, and persevere.
—Maureen Oehler DuRant

For my wife, Nancy, who encourages me in all I do.
—Peter E. Carroll

CONTENTS

Acknowledgments   6

Introduction   7

1.   The War for Independence: Defending the Hudson   9

2.   Stone and Mortar: Building the Academy   21

3.   Chapels: Worshipping at West Point   39

4.   The Long Gray Line: Educating and Training
       the Corps   45

5.   On Brave Old Army Team: Playing Sports and Games   61

6.   The Gloom Period: Weathering West Point Winter   73

7.   Museums and Monuments: Remembering the Past   77

8.   Officers and Gentlemen: Entertaining Friends   87

9.   Three Millions Tourists a Year: Visiting West Point   109

ACKNOWLEDGMENTS

Thank you to the postcard enthusiasts who opened their albums, shared their lifelong collections, and helped create a unique visual history of West Point and its tourism. Col. (Ret.) Seth F. Hudgins Jr., USMA 1964, did not hesitate to graciously offer his amazing collection for use in the book. Roddy MacLeod opened his home on Constitution Island and allowed us to borrow dozens of pieces from his treasure trove. John and June Gunza shared in the excitement of the project and contributed dozens of cards and the knowledge only lifelong collectors could provide. Thank you to Elaine McConnell in the USMA archives who patiently answered questions and provided valuable assistance.

Thank you to my husband, Lt. Col. B. D. DuRant, who always encourages me, gives me great ideas, and gently prods me along the way. Special thanks to my "cadet advisors" Logan Bradley, Peter Choe, Colin DuRant, and David Lee—you guys make me laugh. Thank you to my fellow tour guides at West Point Tours, especially Lori Smith, who enjoys West Point history as much as I do.

Peter would like to acknowledge the people who sparked his passion for collecting postcards and nurtured him in his endeavors. Al Schaut Jr., Patty Moran Ferguson, and Terry Anderson Hover each in their individual way encouraged and guided him on his collecting journey.

—Maureen Oehler DuRant
June 5, 2007

INTRODUCTION

Set in the Highlands along the Hudson River, the scenes of the United States Military Academy at West Point create the perfect picture postcard. The millions of visitors who arrive each year marvel at the vistas, admire the fortresslike architecture, and hope for an opportunity to see a parade or formation. In an attempt to share the experience with friends and family, they purchase postcards, scribble a few lines, and drop them in a mailbox. Those visitors, now numbering up to three million a year, began arriving during the earliest days of the academy. The first postcards printed of West Point were available in local gift shops as early as 1898. In 1906, Eastman Kodak marketed a camera called the "folding pocket camera" and tourists took pictures of scenes and had them printed on the back of postcards. During the golden age of postcards, 1907–1915, postcards gained significant popularity. Collectors kept albums and marveled at the bright beautiful scenes, and a postcard sent from a friend on a holiday was always welcome. Since the first days of postcards, the images preserved time and place, created a historical identity, and promoted the attractions they pictured.

The postcards in this book, primarily from the collection of Peter E. Carroll, preserve specific moments in the history of West Point. Remnants of forts, cannons and mortars, and monuments record the early days of the American War of Independence. Gen. George Washington's generals scouted the Highlands for an advantageous position to defend the critical Hudson River "highway." They chose the west point (the point on the west side of the river) because the Hudson narrows and follows two severe curves. British ships navigating the river would have difficulty maneuvering the turns, slowing down, giving the soldiers at the water batteries time and opportunity for offensive action. Washington commissioned the great chain to be forged and floated on logs across the river to further fortify the position. Through trial and error, threats of betrayal, and hardship in difficult terrain, the Hudson River was held and the Continental army was victorious.

Most postcards sent from West Point picture the buildings, scenes, and cadets of the academy. Thomas Jefferson signed the bill that established the United States Military Academy at the West Point fortress in 1802. Ten cadets, the youngest 10 years old, and five instructors were assigned to begin the school. The academy has grown considerably since that time and now numbers over 4,000 cadets. Women first entered the academy in 1976 and now make up approximately 15 percent of the corps. The postcards in this book demonstrate an evolution of this important American institution: buildings constructed, buildings razed, monuments erected—the academy itself is not a museum. It is a living, working piece of American history. As the corps expands, the academy grows. These postcards record that growth.

Postcards have also contributed to creating a historical identity for West Point. West Point is largely perceived as the institution that "educates, trains, and inspires" the best and brightest of America's sons and daughters. Images of cadets parading are among the favorite postcards collected. The picture of disciplined cadets in beautiful uniforms marching against the backdrop of Washington Hall and the Cadet Chapel causes most Americans to feel proud—proud that young people are willing to serve the country and go to war to preserve its security. At West Point, the buildings and facility itself are not the institution; the graduates of the academy, "the Long Gray Line," form the center of West Point's character.

Historically businesses and institutions have used postcards for self-promotion. Although the academy licenses images for use, it is not in the souvenir business. Local gift shops, however, take the opportunity to offer memorabilia and, of course, postcards. The Daughters of the United States Army (DUSA), which operates the gift shop in the museum has produced West Point postcards since it began operating 40 years ago—the proceeds generated in the DUSA shop are given away in scholarships and donations to the community. Highland Falls businesses, such as B. Rose Hardware and Golden's Gift Shop (now Vasily's), also sold (and continue to sell) postcards. Formal tours of the academy officially started in 1947, when West Point Tours began operation. Of course, residents of the academy grounds and cadets have always shown their guests the sights at West Point. Today guided bus tours leave the visitors' information center almost every day of the year.

The fortifications at West Point contributed significantly to winning the Revolutionary War. The thousands of cadets who have graduated from United States Military Academy served and died in every war our nation has fought to preserve that freedom. The cadets who train at United States Military Academy are becoming part of that legacy. When tourists see West Point, they come to understand the critical importance of this special place as a significant Revolutionary War site and the home of the nation's oldest and largest military academy. The history of postcards parallels the history of West Point and of that tourism that followed. This place, majestic and extraordinary, is truly "as pretty as a postcard."

One

THE WAR FOR INDEPENDENCE

DEFENDING THE HUDSON

VIEW OF HUDSON RIVER FROM TROPHY POINT. The defenses and the soldiers who were stationed at West Point during the Revolutionary War secured the victory for the American cause. The United States Military Academy (USMA) established at that same fort in 1802 "educated, trained, and inspired" the men and women who defended the freedom won and continue to defend this great nation. (Courtesy of John and June Gunza.)

VIEW OF CHAPEL AND PLAIN FROM TROPHY POINT. Gen. George Washington and his strategists (and certainly the British) recognized the critical importance of the Hudson River to success in the Revolutionary War. Despite the attempt at sabotage by Gen. Benedict Arnold, the defenses at West Point secured the river and the ultimate victory. Before, during, and after the war, Congress debated the need for a military academy. Washington advised that "However pacific the general policy of a nation may be, it ought never to be without an adequate stock of military knowledge . . . for this purpose an academy where a regular course of instruction is given is an obvious expedient."

WASHINGTON'S MONUMENT. Washington's monument, sculpted by Henry Kirke Brown and unveiled in 1916, now (it seems to have roamed the post) stands directly in front of Washington Hall in the cadet area. Noted for his equestrian statues, Brown also sculpted statues of Gen. Winfield Scott located in Washington, D.C., and another of Washington located in Union Square Park, New York City. Buried in the West Point Cemetery, Scott fought alongside academy graduates in the Mexican War and issued his famous "Scott's Fixed Opinion," a statement praising the officers of the academy.

REAR VIEW, WASHINGTON MONUMENT. Washington's monument is often the recipient of good-humored cadet fun. During graduation week, the monument may wear graduation robes and a mortarboard. Over time, the monument has development a green patina. One evening a group of cadets decided to "polish" the private parts of the horse. The cadets were discovered and duly punished for the prank—they were required to pay restoration fees and walk hours on the area. (Courtesy of John and June Gunza.)

AERIAL VIEW OF WEST POINT. The British strategies included a strike from the north from New York and south from Lake Champlain, seizing control of the Hudson and cutting the colonies in half. To win the war, the Continental Congress agreed that the Hudson River must be secured. After surveying several sites, Christopher Tappan and James Clinton determined that the severe turns and narrow passage combined with a swift tide and high winds at West Point provided the most advantageous defensive position. This aerial view looking north clearly shows that topography.

View down Hudson River, from the Bend at West Point.

WEST POINT LIGHTHOUSES ON THE HUDSON RIVER. Since West Point is the Hudson's most dangerous place on the river owing to strong currents and difficult topography, lighthouses provided an essential navigational component for the busy river traffic. Floods wreaked havoc on the lighthouses, and none have survived.

Copyrighted 1906 by B. & S.
Light House at West Point, N. Y.

No. B-5 Barton & Spooner, Cornwall-on-Hudson, N. Y. (Printed in Germany)

WEST POINT LIGHTHOUSE. A series of lighthouses at West Point was located on Gee's Point. This hexagonal tower replaced the original West Point Light in 1872. A schooner ran ashore and destroyed the fog bell tower in 1921. Note the picnicking visitors on the rocks.

12

Kosciuszko's Monument. Washington appointed Col. Tadeusz Kosciuszko, a Polish officer who volunteered for the American cause, to supervise construction of the fortifications at West Point following several attempts made by other officers. In 1780, Washington named Kosciuszko chief of the engineering corps. A wreath-laying ceremony celebrating Kosciuszko's birthday takes place each year. (Courtesy of Roddy MacLeod.)

Kosciuszko's Garden. In his leisure time, Kosciuszko erected a beautiful garden and foundation located behind Memorial Hall. On a granite ledge above the garden, the word *Saratoga* is carved into the stone. In 1857, Maj. Richard Delafield directed that the names of three major Revolutionary War battles be inscribed on rock ledges throughout West Point. He intended the memorials to be lasting reminders to the cadets. (Courtesy of John and June Gunza.)

13

KOSCIUSKO'S MONUMENT.

WEST POINT FROM FORT PUTNAM.

KOSCIUSZKO'S ORIGINAL MONUMENT, VIEW FROM FORT PUTNAM. After reading the Declaration of Independence, Kosciuszko was moved to tears and determined to meet Thomas Jefferson. The two men became lifelong friends. The corps erected the pedestal of the monument in 1828, and the Polish clergy and laity in the United States presented the statue in 1913.

LINKS FROM THE GREAT CHAIN. On Trophy Point, 13 links (one for each colony) of the great chain serve as a monument to the 500-yard-long iron chain used as a defensive Revolutionary War fortification. Each spring for four years, soldiers hauled the chain across the Hudson, floating it on log rafts, hauling it back when ice began to form. Forged at Sterling Ironwork in Warwick, the Continental soldiers called it "General Washington's watch chain." After the war, the valuable iron was sent to the West Point Foundry furnaces. Several unscrupulous entrepreneurs sold counterfeit sections of the chain after the war as valuable mementoes. The only authentic links, however, are found at West Point. The effectiveness of the chain is still under debate, but the British never attempted to break it; so, in the end, it worked.

MAGAZINE POINT ON CONSTITUTION ISLAND. Soldiers attached the great chain to capstans on either side of the river. The terrain in this area of the Highlands is difficult, and the Continental army thought it was largely impervious to British attack. Before it was totally secured, however, British forces overran the island. After occupying the island for a time, the British withdrew and patriot forces rebuilt the fortifications, concentrating the efforts at West Point.

CONSTITUTION ISLAND. American army engineers first concentrated their defensive efforts at Martelaer's Rock, later known as Constitution Fort and then Constitution Island. The British captured the island in 1777 on their way to Saratoga. After it reverted to the Americans, the army constructed three redoubts (a fort used to protect soldiers outside of a larger fort), a barracks, and a water battery, which defended the chain.

GARDEN WALK. After the war, Henry Warner, a lawyer from Long Island, acquired the island. Purportedly he brought a briefcase loaded with $50,000 cash for the purchase. Although he had plans to develop the island into a resort, financial disaster forced him and his two daughters, Anna and Susan, to live year-round on the island's 280 acres. Gardening helped alleviate the isolation of the island, and the sisters spent time tending flowers and vegetables. The flower gardens, now designated historical gardens, are maintained by volunteers.

WARNER FAMILY HOME. The two sisters spent long lonely hours on the island gardening. The Constitution Island Association and caretaker Roddy MacLeod maintain the home and grounds. Tours are available during the summer months. Unlike her older sister, Anna Warner relished the natural beauty of their "rock" and, as a small girl, explored the deserted forts and enjoyed the solitude. She wrote a book that reflected her love of gardening, titled *Gardening by Myself,* but is most known for penning the words to the hymn "Jesus Loves Me."

REAR VIEW OF WARNER HOME. One wall of the Warner home dates from the Revolutionary War era. The family lived in dire financial straits, and to keep their belongings from being auctioned off in the sheriff's sales, the Warner sisters wrote prolifically. Susan Warner wrote under the pen name Elizabeth Wetherell. Critics describe her best seller, *A Wide, Wide World* (1851), as a female "Huck Finn." Although the book was enormously popular, copyright laws were not effectual and she did not collect royalties.

CLOSE-UP VIEW, WARNER HOME. The sisters lived out their lives on the island, teaching Bible studies to cadets who were happy to escape the rigors of West Point for a few hours. Their "man of all work" rowed across the river and rowed back with the cadets. "Miss Warner's boys," as the cadets came to be called, enjoyed gingerbread and tea. The house contains much of the original furnishings and personal family effects.

Constitution Island.

Old Fort, Easterly side of the Island. War of Independence.

REVOLUTIONARY WAR FORT ON CONSTITUTION ISLAND. The remains of several old forts are scattered throughout the island, and trails provide pleasant hikes for visitors. Determined that the island become part of the West Point military reservation, Anna Warner refused several offers to sell the property for large sums of money. In 1908, Anna's wishes became reality when Margaret Olivia Slocum Sage, wife of Russell Sage, purchased the island and deeded it to the U.S. government.

OUTSIDE WALL OF FORT PUTNAM. Built in 1778 by the 5th Massachusetts Regiment under the direction of Col. Rufus Putnam, Fort Putnam protected the forward batteries and redoubts in a system of fortifications defending the river. Owing to the rocky terrain and steep climbs, the fort was considered impregnable and held enough supplies to withstand a 10-day siege.

INSIDE FORT PUTNAM. The fort, with its brick-arched casements (vaulted chambers), purportedly cost $35,000 of the $3 million spent to secure the Highlands. Supplied with 450 troops and 14 mounted guns, the fort became the key fortification in the elaborate system of batteries, redoubts, and forts. Dismantled in 1787, it was rebuilt entirely of stone and brick in 1794.

VIEW FROM FORT PUTNAM. Although no battles were ever fought at Fort Putnam, it has come to symbolize the War of Independence to visitors at West Point. The fort was restored during the Revolutionary War's bicentennial and opened to the public; school groups and historians take advantage of seasonal openings and limited hours. Reproduction cannons and mortars were placed according to the original plans by Lt. Louis-Alexandre Berthier, a Revolutionary War topographic engineer. After a hike to the summit, 500 feet above sea level, visitors are rewarded by some of the most striking views of the river and mountains on West Point. On very clear days, the Catskill Mountains may come into view. Thomas Cole, of the Hudson River School, reproduced the scene beautifully when he painted *View of Fort Putnam*.

Two

STONE AND MORTAR
BUILDING THE ACADEMY

THOMAS JEFFERSON PORTRAIT. The United States Military Academy at West Point was founded in 1802 under the presidency of Thomas Jefferson. The officer and cadets at the academy commissioned the portrait that now hangs in the West Point Museum. The portrait is by noted artist Thomas Sully.

ADMINISTRATION BUILDING. Prior to the expansion of the West Point, Taylor Hall (also known as the administration building) stood as a sentinel at the gateway to the fortress. Built by the architect Ralph Adams Cram, sculptor Lee Lawrie decorated the building with ornate stone carvings. Budget constraints ceased work on the carvings, and when Lawrie was engaged to finish one of the larger eagles, he declared that nature had completed it while it was left unattended. He finished the large Athena carving above the library entrance just before his death in 1963. The 160-foot masonry tower houses offices.

TAYLOR HALL. Legend says that second-class cadets (juniors) are referred to as cows because in the early days of the academy the first leave was granted the summer after sophomore year. As they would return up the hill, the upperclassmen would stand at the arch and remark to one another, "The cows are returning to the barn all fattened up from pasture."

ACADEMIC BOARDROOM, TAYLOR HALL. Sculptor Lee Lawrie carved the large, stone fireplace located in the academic boardroom in Taylor Hall. The mantel displays nine figures: Joshua, Hector, David, Alexander the Great, Julius Caesar, Charlemagne, King Arthur, Godfrey de Bouillon, and Judas Maccabeus. William Caxton's preface to Thomas Malory's *Morte d'Arthur* inspired the choice of figures. The heads of the academic department have reserved seats around the enormous conference table and meet periodically to review cadet performances. (Courtesy of John and June Gunza.)

23

GRANT HALL. This postcard pictures the old Grant Hall, which served as the cadet mess. It was named for Pres. Ulysses S. Grant, USMA 1843. During his tenure as a cadet he went home to Ohio for leave. Later he wrote, "Those ten weeks were shorter than one week at West Point." Today's cadets have the same feeling.

CADETS AT DINNER, INTERIOR OF GRANT HALL. Cadets are still served as depicted on this postcard. Seated at tables for 10, cadets are served family style by waiters. Plebes (first-year cadets) seated at the table must perform table duties, which include pouring coffee and other beverages, and announcing ("Sir, the dessert today is chocolate cake. How many at the table would like cake?"), cutting, and serving dessert. Dessert must be divided evenly, and when odd numbers are required, nervous plebes may use templates to guide the cutting.

24

RECEPTION ROOM IN GRANT HALL. The "new" Grant Hall is used as a snack bar for cadets and guests. Professors may take classes to Grant Hall for informal lessons. Paintings of the U.S. Army's five-star generals (Arnold, Bradley, Eisenhower, Marshall, and MacArthur) adorn the walls. All but Marshall graduated from West Point—he went to the Virginia Military Institute.

HEADQUARTERS, LIBRARY, RIDING HALL. Beginning in 1839, cadets were taught equitation. The old riding hall is pictured on the right side of this card. Thayer Hall took its place. Although Ulysses S. Grant attained mediocre standing in academics and found life at West Point "interminable," he excelled in horsemanship skills. James Longstreet, USMA 1842, said of Grant, "in horsemanship, however, he was noted as the most proficient in the Academy. In fact, rider and horse held together like the fabled centaur." Grant's skills did not, however, earn him a coveted U.S. Calvary assignment.

ENTRANCE TO THAYER HALL. Horsemanship skills were deleted from the curriculum in the 1940s, and a renovation of Thayer Hall provided much-needed academic space. In 1955, the interior was completely gutted and four floors of classrooms were constructed. Details such as several architectural sculptures adorn the building and provide a hint of the building's past use.

VIEW FROM THE RIVER. The views from the river show a granite and limestone fortress that seems to emerge seamlessly from the stone. The train tunnel is three-fifths of a mile long and runs beneath the plain and emerges on the other side of Trophy Point. Although passenger travel ended on the west side of the river, the freight trains pass up to 52 times per day.

OFFICER'S MESS HALL, WEST POINT, N. Y.

OFFICERS' MESS HALL. Built in 1903 for $103,000, the officers' quarters and mess is now the West Point Club. When first built, it housed 30 or so bachelor officers and offered dining and a "club house." At one point it served as the West Point Officer's Club. Today very few officers' clubs exist on military installations; most have evolved into community clubs.

Memorial Building, West Point, N. Y.

MEMORIAL HALL. Brevet Maj. Gen. George W. Cullum, USMA 1933, willed $250,000 to complete Memorial Hall, or Cullum Hall, a beautiful building of Milford pink granite. The purpose of the building is to house and display the memorials to distinguished graduates of the academy. The large cannons at the entrance are trophies from Santiago deCuba.

BALLROOM IN CULLUM HALL. This postcard shows the second floor of the building, a massive ballroom. A frieze encircles the room and lists the names of battles from the War of 1812 to the Spanish-American War of 1898. Bronze plaques inscribed with the names of graduates who have died in service to the country are hung throughout the halls.

RIVERVIEW FROM CULLUM HALL. The roofed open gallery running the full length on the back on Cullum Hall provides a spectacular view of the Hudson. Visitors can walk down a staircase to Kocciuszko's garden, a shady site with a foundation built by Kocciuszko during his tenure at West Point. As part of plebe knowledge, a plebe may be asked "How many lights in Cullum Hall?" To which he replies, "Sir, 340 lights." (Courtesy of Col. [Ret.] Seth Hudgins, USMA 1964.)

CULLUM HALL. Historic postcards may be dated by several characteristics: the style of postcard, the postmark (not always an indicator since postcards may or may not have been mailed when they were purchased), and the details in the picture itself. Clothing styles, specific buildings, and other details reveal the age of the photograph. This postcard is a "linen" postcard, characterized by visible, slightly coarse lines resembling a linen texture throughout the card. The cards were inexpensively produced and are also known for their bright coloring. Linen postcards are dated 1930–1945. The old car pictured also hints at the period.

OLD LIBRARY. Built of native granite in 1841, the old library was destroyed to make way for the new library built in 1964. A fixture on the plain and in the lives of cadets for over 100 years, architects remodeled the library in 1900, but it still could not keep up with the expanding needs of the growing academy. A new library and media center, Jefferson Hall, will provide expansive spaces and technological support for a modern university.

West Point, N.Y. Cadet Hospital, U.S. Military Academy.

CADET HOSPITAL. Built in 1875, the cadet hospital stood on the site that now occupies the administration building. Like many of the other buildings, architects used local granite to erect the structure. Keller Army Hospital, located on the northwest section of post, now serves the needs of cadets and military personnel assigned to West Point.

Two Academic Buildings, West Point, N.Y.

CLOCK TOWER. The clock tower abuts Pershing Barracks in the cadet area. On a spirit mission a band of cadets disassembled the reveille cannon late one night, transported it to the clock tower, and reassembled it. Academy engineers took over two weeks to return it to its position on the plain. The reveille cannon is now bolted in its place overlooking the Hudson on Trophy Point.

WASHINGTON HALL. Standing majestically at the center of the parade field, the original section of Washington Hall was built in 1929. The building houses the mess hall, kitchen facilities, offices, and classrooms. Four thousand cadets march up the steps into the mess hall three times per day where they are served family style by an efficient staff of waiters and cooks. A team of nutritionists carefully attend to the specific dietary needs of cadets. Cooks prepare food on multiple levels, complete with cold kitchens for salads; hot kitchens for meats, soups, and sauces; a bakery; and pantries.

OLD LIBRARY AND TREES. The trees that line the plain and Trophy Point area are marked as class gifts. During the Revolutionary era, all trees on both sides of the rivers were taken down for building, for firewood, and to clear the line of sight to the river. The trees are replaced as needed.

NEW SOUTH BARRACK WING AND GUARD HOUSE.   WEST POINT, N. Y.

CENTRAL AREA. The open courtyard between barracks form Central Area. Few cadets escape "walking the area" during their tenure at West Point. A form of punishment, walking the area involves marching in platoon formation for an assigned number of hours. The "walking," done in full-dress uniform under arms, is completed in a cadet's free time. A cadet who marches 100 hours or more is known as a "century man."

WEST POINT·N·Y· 41.

VIEW THROUGH SALLY PORT. This real–photo postcard looks through a sally port into Central Area. During inclement weather, cadets may drill or have formations under the cover of the sally ports. As the regiment files onto the field for dress parade, they form in the cadet areas and stream through the sally ports onto the parade field. Most of the West Point real–photo postcards that were circulated can be attributed to William H. Stockbridge, an official photographer for the academy. Many other postcard images are also Stockbridge's work. Stockbridge completed most of his work during the 1920s and 1930s. His full collection is in the wonderful USMA archives. The Cadet Chapel is on the hill above. (Courtesy of Col. [Ret.] Seth Hudgins, USMA 1964.)

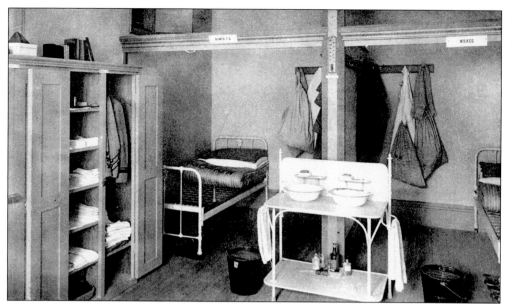

CADET ROOM. Although the furnishings and fixtures are updated, the cadets currently attending West Point still must keep their rooms in perfect order. Most new cadets make their beds to standard and then just sleep on top of the blanket to save time in the mornings. This practice, although widely used and quite effective, is not condoned by their superiors. Cadets typically share a room with one or two others in their class. Roommates generally become lifelong friends. (Courtesy of Col. [Ret.] Seth Hudgins, USMA 1964.)

SOUTH BARRACKS. South Barracks was built in 1850 of local granite. When built, it contained 200 rooms, each 14 by 22 feet. Two cadets were assigned to each room. Most barracks are named for general officers who have graduated from West Point. There are Grant, Lee, Pershing, Bradley, and Sherman Barracks, among others. Although visitors are strictly prohibited from entering the barracks, parents are offered an opportunity to view rooms during Plebe Parent Weekend.

NORTH BARRACKS. North Barracks, completed in 1908, provided much-needed rooms for the expanding corps. Again native granite, sandstone, and brick were used. When built, it cost $230,000. Formations and inspections take place in front of the barracks before mandatory meals. During football season, clever spirit signs hang outside the windows.

EAST AND WEST ACADEMIC BUILDINGS. Completed in 1895 by architect Richard Morris Hunt, the academic building project seemed doomed from the start. Budget considerations and problems with contractors delayed the project for several years. Eventually it housed classrooms for law, mathematics, engineering, and other academic subjects. Drawing, a required course for cadets, occupied the entire fourth floor. James McNeil Whistler, although dismissed for failing chemistry, excelled in drawing, and many of his sketches of cadets are retained in the archives.

PROFESSOR'S ROW. Quarters 100 and 101 are virtually unrecognizable in this early postcard (postmarked 1911). Quarters 100, built for the superintendent of USMA in 1819, has undergone extensive and numerous alterations and renovations throughout the years. Every superintendent since Sylvanus Thayer has lived in the home, and most U.S. presidents have been guests. (Courtesy of Col. [Ret.] Seth Hudgins, USMA 1964.)

SUPERINTENDENT'S QUARTERS. The architecture of Quarters 100 was originally a basic rectangular Federal-style home. The porch was added in the 1930s. The superintendent's staff includes a chef and his assistant. Dozens of events take place in the home each year, including large dinner parties and receptions. Over the years visitors have presented gifts to the superintendent that remain in the house. (Courtesy of John and June Gunza.)

GATE TO THE GARDENS OF QUARTERS 100.
The beautiful gardens adjoining Quarters 100 contain plantings from all 50 states. Cadet parent clubs contributed perennials, shrubs, and trees to the garden. Not all survived the cold winters. Painstakingly maintained, the gardens are opened several times throughout the year for entertaining and tours. (Courtesy of Col. [Ret.] Seth Hudgins, USMA 1964.)

The Hudson River from Officers' Quarters, West Point, N.Y.

VIEW FROM OFFICER'S QUARTERS. An assignment to West Point is generally considered to be quite advantageous. Most officers earn a master's degree or doctorate before the assignment, and the post is one of the most beautiful in the army. Some officers are lucky enough to draw quarters with a view of the Hudson River, a most desirable feature. (Courtesy of Col. [Ret.] Seth Hudgins, USMA 1964.)

THAYER ROAD QUARTERS. Built by the architectural firm Cram, Goodhue, and Ferguson in 1908, these homes built above Thayer Road were originally intended for captains and lieutenants. The seven houses represent some of the most beautiful homes on post. Finished in the arts and crafts style, the interiors vary from house to house, but all feature spectacular woodwork. (Courtesy of John and June Gunza.)

ENLISTED MEN'S HOSPITAL. Originally constructed as a hospital for enlisted men in 1891, this building later became a military police barracks. In 1936, a major renovation converted the building into three homes for officers. The large wrap-around porch served as a recuperation area for invalids. (Courtesy of John and June Gunza.)

Three

CHAPELS
WORSHIPPING AT WEST POINT

CHAPEL. Originally situated on the plain between the clock tower and cadet library, the Greek Revival Old Cadet Chapel was built in 1837. After construction of the new chapel in 1910, plans to demolish the old chapel were met by the alumni's passionate objections. In 1910, it was moved block by block to its current location in the West Point Cemetery. The mural *War and Peace* by Robert Weir fills the wall above the altar. A collection of shields commemorating Revolutionary War generals adorns the west wall of the interior of the chapel. A name is absent on one shield: Benedict Arnold.

OLD CADET CHAPEL. The Old Cadet Chapel, known as the Mortuary Chapel, houses a columbarium in the undercroft. In the early days of the cemetery, bodies were lowered into the basement by an elevator in the main floor of the chapel. During the winter, they could be kept in temporary vaults until the ground thawed and graves could be dug. On the west wall of the chapel are plaques bearing the names of graduates killed in the Mexican War and Indian wars. A plaque commemorating the first graduating class of 1802 is also displayed. Fifty percent of the class of 1802 was Jewish (there were two graduates). Jewish cadets worshipped in the Old Cadet Chapel until the completion of the Jewish chapel in 1984.

MOST HOLY TRINITY CATHOLIC CHAPEL. Built in 1900, the Catholic chapel is almost an exact replica of the Abbey Church of St. Ethelreda in Essex, England. The Catholic chapel was the first Roman Catholic church built on government property, and the church retained ownership until 2000, when the academy assumed care and ownership.

INTERIOR, CATHOLIC CHAPEL. The interior of the Most Holy Trinity Catholic Chapel has gone through many changes. Painted scenes now adorn the exposed beams, and a dramatic carved crucifix is above the altar. Beautiful Tiffany windows depicting saints with military associations adorn the interior. Windows also memorialize Catholic graduates who have fallen in action. This postcard shows the original black-and-white tile floor. (Courtesy of Col. [Ret.] Seth Hudgins, USMA 1964.)

CADET CHAPEL. As the corps expanded, the need for a larger chapel prompted an architectural competition for the contract to complete the building. The firm of Cram, Goodhue, and Ferguson won the contract and produced the imposing Military Gothic structure in 1910. Although the academy asked for a chapel in the cadet area, the architects choose the commanding site on the hill above—an inspired move.

41

CADET CHAPEL AND OBSERVATORY. The chapel exterior is adorned with architectural ornamentation by sculptor Lee Lawrie. The cross above the chapel door represents Excalibur, and the figures surrounding the chapel are from the Arthurian legends in search of the Holy Grail. In this postcard, the old observatory can be seen behind the chapel.

INTERIOR, CADET CHAPEL. The windows in the chapel were designed and executed by the Willet Stained Glass and Decorating Studios of Philadelphia. The great chancel window was selected in a competition, winning over Tiffany. The limestone altar, a gift from the family of Ulysses S. Grant, USMA 1843, shows St. Michael slaying a dragon. The Cadet Chapel Choir leads the music and worship. When Norman Schwarzkopf Jr., USMA 1956, attended West Point he led the chapel choir. (Courtesy of Col. [Ret.] Seth Hudgins, USMA 1964.)

FLAGS IN CADET CHAPEL. The aisle in the Cadet Chapel is over 100 feet long—quite a distance for a bride to walk. A door on the side midway down the aisle is referred to as the "bride's escape." (In a Gothic chapel, the side door represents the wound in Christ's side when he was on the cross.) Since cadets are not allowed to be married, quite a few weddings take place in the chapel following graduation. Although men most always get married in uniform, female graduates usually choose a traditional wedding dress. According to the chaplains, no bride has yet to use the escape route.

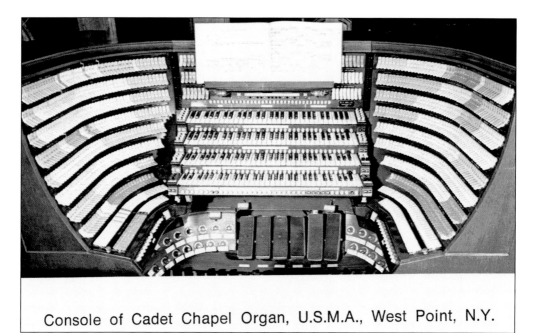

Console of Cadet Chapel Organ, U.S.M.A., West Point, N.Y.

CONSOLE OF CADET CHAPEL ORGAN. The chapel houses the world's largest church pipe organ. Enlarged through private donations, the organ's over 23,000 pipes are tuned and maintained by a full-time curator and associate. The console pictured brings together the organist's skill with the pipes hidden throughout the building. West Point Chapel organist Craig Williams conducts the Cadet Chapel Choir.

CRYPT, CADET CHAPEL. Twelve crypts in the undercroft of the Cadet Chapel remain empty. St. Martin's Eastern Orthodox Chapel now occupies this area. Cadets refer to a room under the north side of the chapel as "the dungeon." A meeting hall is also housed in the undercroft. (Courtesy of John and June Gunza.)

Four

THE LONG GRAY LINE
EDUCATING AND TRAINING THE CORPS

THAYER MONUMENT. Sylvanus Thayer, USMA 1808, is known as the "Father of the United States Military Academy." He held the position of superintendent from 1817 to 1833. During his tenure, he instituted a formal plan of study centering on applied engineering, enforced strict discipline, and laid the foundation for the honor code. Cadets openly rebelled against the new restrictions and to this day when enduring a difficult week they may comment, "It's a Thayer Week." The white granite statue, sculpted by Carl Conrad, was erected in 1883.

RECEPTION DAY. The new cadets present themselves on Reception Day, known as R-Day. After a brief goodbye to friends and relatives, the new cadets are whisked away to endure a long arduous day culminating in their first parade and the "swearing in" ceremony on Trophy Point. Anxious parents look for their new cadet, who is often unrecognizable after the military haircut, regulation army glasses, and uniform—not to mention the somber expression. (Courtesy of Col. [Ret.] Seth Hudgins, USMA 1964.)

NEW CADET CANDIDATES. Today's new cadets typically show up in shorts or jeans but wearing the broken-in black low quarters (shoes) as instructed. Their civilian attire is quickly replaced by uniforms, and "Beast Barracks" (cadet basic training) has officially begun. The cadets arrive from all 50 states and from many allied nations around the world. The class begins with approximately 1,300 new cadets. (Courtesy of Col. [Ret.] Seth Hudgins, USMA 1964.)

PLEBE RECOGNITION. Plebes are officially recognized at graduation. (The date of recognition has varied throughout the years.) Recognition means an end to fourth-class status, and with rank comes privilege, including an additional pass, the right to "fall-out" (constant state of attention, hands cupped, eyes forward, rendering proper greetings to upperclassmen, and no talking in the cadet area—falling-out means an end to these requirements), and calling upperclassmen by their first names.

ROAD MARCH. Road marches have always been a part of military training and continue today. During Beast Barracks, new cadets perform several road marches, each longer than the last. The summer culminates with a 12- to 15-mile road march to West Point from training areas. As the new cadets march into post, family members and well-wishers cheer their accomplishment.

MESS IN THE FIELD. The old adage "an army travels on its stomach" is a fundamental concept in the army. Keeping soldiers well fed is critical to keeping morale high. Today's mess in the field generally consists of meals ready to eat (MREs), a waterproof package of food, condiments (hot sauce is always included), a flameless heater, and utensils. Some of the less-popular meals have earned nicknames like "Meals Rejected by Everyone."

"Policing Camp, West Point, N. Y.

POLICING CAMP. Plebes are assigned the responsibility for policing specific areas. Other duties assigned to plebes include laundry pickup and delivery, cleaning latrines, and calling minutes—plebes stand at attention at intervals in the hallways of the barracks and call out the minutes before formations, the uniform of the day, and any other pertinent orders.

SUMMER CAMP. The caption on the back of this card reads, "During the summer, the entire battalion of cadets at the West Point Military Academy go into camp in tents some distance from the Academy buildings. The camp is regularly laid out in streets (by companies), and one of these thoroughfares with a sentry on guard is shown in this illustration."

BRIDGE BUILDING. USMA is considered the oldest engineering school in the United States. Congress, in the establishment of the academy, determined that the need for officers would not be a constant demand; therefore training engineers would be beneficial to the country. West Point engineers were largely responsible for building the infrastructure for the nation. They designed and built bridges, roads, and railroad lines.

INTERIOR, THAYER HALL, RIDING PRACTICE. USMA began cavalry training in 1839. Cadets often gave demonstrations of great skill and daring to onlookers seated in the gallery in the hall. (Courtesy of Col. [Ret.] Seth Hudgins, USMA 1964.)

INTERIOR, RIDING ACADEMY. After World War II, the army began to run on gasoline instead of hay. The academy began to teach motor vehicle instruction in its place. Cadets at West Point are now afforded the opportunity to drive High Mobility Multipurpose Wheeled Vehicles (HMMWVs or Humvees), quite the change from horses.

MOUNTED GYMNASTICS. The back of this postcard reads, "The regular cavalry detachment on duty at West Point, as well as the cadets, are noted for their excellent horsemanship. Bare-back riding and other exercises are a feature of their routine work."

MOUNTAIN BATTERY PRACTICE. Mountain batteries carried gun parts, ammunition, and supplies on horseback. Mules and other animals were also employed. The drills practiced packing and unpacking as well as assembling the guns and target practice.

OLD RIDING HALL. After the riding hall was completed in 1846, cadets practiced horsemanship skills all year. George B. McClellan, USMA 1846, designed a riding saddle that was adopted by the army in 1859. Today the saddle is used in ceremonial mounts, including the historic Field Artillery Half Section at Fort Sill, Oklahoma.

LIGHT ARTILLERY DRILL. Formed in 1858, the Department of Tactics answered a need for experience in the advances in weaponry. Currently cadets learn advanced field training in the summer between their first and second year. Cadet field training (CFT) takes place at Camp Buckner with one-week rotation at Fort Knox, Kentucky.

SIGNAL PRACTICE. Practical training in all the combat arms and combat arms support branches has always been taught at the academy. During their third year at the academy, cadets participate in Military Individual Advanced Development training courses such as Air Assault; Airborne; Mountain Warfare; Northern Warfare; Special Reaction Team Course, Sapper Leader; and Survival, Evasion, Resistance, and Escape (SERE) training courses. (Courtesy of John and June Gunza.)

ARTILLERY ON THE MARCH. Scenes such as the one on this postcard are reminiscent of the Civil War. Robert Anderson, USMA 1826, defended Fort Sumter against Pierre G. T. Beauregard, USMA 1838. Anderson had taught Beauregard field artillery at West Point. Beauregard served as superintendent for five days before he was relieved for "Southern sympathies."

ARTILLERY DRILLS. The instruction for "standing gun drill" included loading and firing a field cannon and mounting and dismounting the cannon and carriage. Field artillery, considered a military science, has been called the "King of the Battlefield" because of its destructive force. After graduation, cadets entering the field artillery branch complete their officer basic course at Fort Sill, Oklahoma, where they are taught advanced tactics, techniques, and procedures for the use of fire support systems.

Artillery Drill, West Point, N. Y.

RAPID FIRE GUN DRILL. A monument in the West Point Cemetery, the Cadet Monument, memorializes cadet Vincent M. Lowe. Lowe was killed in artillery practice on January 1, 1817, when the cannon discharged prematurely. Every member of the corps donated $15 toward erecting the monument.

DISAPPEARING GUNS. Disappearing guns, artillery primarily used on coastal areas, could be lowered into a bunker. They could be easily concealed from the enemy. The United States continued to use the guns through World War II. Prior to the acquisition of training areas outside the main post, artillery practice took place at batteries close to the Hudson River.

ROUGH-RIDING. Although an average student, cadet Ulysses S. Grant excelled in horsemanship skills. Cadet James Longstreet said that Grant was "the most daring horseman at the Academy." He was a very handsome man, and all who watched admired his skill. At graduation, Grant was singled out to demonstrate jumping. His record jump stood for 25 years. He married his roommate's sister, also an accomplished horsewoman. Their son, Frederick Dent Grant, USMA 1871, is buried in the West Point Cemetery.

ARTILLERY BARRACKS. The artillery barracks and stables were built in 1903 by the architectural firm of Cram, Goodhue, and Ferguson. The academy suspended horsemanship skills during the Civil War. Instruction began again shortly after the war was over and finally ended with the mechanization of the military. The facades of the buildings are virtually original. The function of the buildings, however, has changed significantly. The old stables now house offices, the post library, and a bowling alley. (Courtesy of Col. [Ret.] Seth Hudgins, USMA 1964.)

Artillery Barracks and Stables West Point, N. Y.

INTERIOR, ARTILLERY BARRACKS. This postcard picturing the interior of the artillery barracks clearly depicts the spartan living conditions of single soldiers. The quality of life for single soldiers has improved throughout the years with the addition of larger barracks, single–soldier clubs, and recreational facilities. (Courtesy of John and June Gunza.)

CAVALRY BARRACKS. In 1907, African American soldiers from the 9th and 10th U.S. Cavalry Regiments were assigned to teach riding instruction and mounted drill. The soldiers served on the American frontier and were dubbed "Buffalo Soldiers" by the Native Americans. The unit was deactivated in 1946. The field in front of the stables, formerly called Cavalry Plain, was renamed Buffalo Soldier Field in honor of those soldiers.

MODERN CLASSROOM. Col. Sylvanus Thayer introduced "the Thayer Method" of instruction at West Point. Classes are small, and cadets are required to prepare for each class. Given the command "take boards," cadets take places at the boards (now mostly whiteboards) and present the lesson and respond to questions posed by the instructor.

AFTER A PARADE. This real-photo postcard scene shows cadets shaking hands after a parade. The "goat," the cadet with the lowest academic average, of the class receives special recognition from his classmates. Traditionally each new lieutenant shakes his hand and gives him a silver dollar. In the early days of the academy, a professor with a goatee taught the cadets at the bottom of the class—hence those students were called "goats." Some famous goats over the years have included George Armstrong Custer, USMA 1861, and George Pickett, USMA 1846.

GRADUATION ON TROPHY POINT. After graduation, cadets are commissioned into the regular army as second lieutenants where they begin to serve an eight-year military obligation. Graduation now takes place in Michie Stadium and ends with the hat toss. It is considered bad luck to pick up one's hat, so the field is left littered with the white hats as the new lieutenants leave the stadium. Cadets often put money or notes in the "service caps" they have worn for four years. Children in the stands are allowed to pick up hats for souvenirs and walk around afterward sporting their new headgear—perhaps a reflection of the future?

Five

ON BRAVE OLD
ARMY TEAM
PLAYING SPORTS AND GAMES

MACARTHUR MONUMENT. While serving as superintendent of West Point (1919–1922), Douglas MacArthur, USMA 1903, further expanded the formal athletic program. His often-quoted lines "Upon the fields of friendly strife are sown the seeds that, upon others fields, on other days, will bear the fruits of victory" are the basis for physical education at West Point. He believed that team sports promoted opportunities to learn quick decision-making at critical moments, perseverance in difficult circumstances, and most importantly, teamwork—all skills imperative to great leadership.

AERIAL VIEW, MICHIE STADIUM. The army football field in Michie Stadium provides the backdrop for spirited home games. Situated above Lusk Reservoir, the fans in the upper decks enjoy views of the Hudson River and the post's incredible fall foliage. Firsties (seniors) from the Army Parachute Team drop into the stadium with the American flag, USCC (United States Corps of Cadets) flag, the POW/MIA flag, and the game ball.

BLAIK FIELD. The field is named for Earl "Red" Blaik, the most winning coach in the history of army football. Blaik coached the army team to three national championships. Buried in the West Point cemetery next to the old chapel, Blaik's football–shaped gravestone is inscribed: "On Brave Old Army Team." (Courtesy of Roddy MacLeod.)

ARMY GAME, MICHIE STADIUM. The football team is escorted to the field by bagpipers while the crowd erupts in cheers. The entire corps of cadets attends the games in uniform, standing ready in support of the team on the field. After each score, the cadets rush to the field to do pushups—one for each point. (Courtesy of Col. [Ret.] Seth Hudgins, USMA 1964.)

EAST VIEW, MICHIE STADIUM. The stadium is named for Dennis Mahan Michie, USMA 1892, who contrived to bring football to West Point. Through determination and cunning, he convinced the leadership at West Point that a challenge by the naval academy must not go unanswered. Only a handful of cadets had ever played the game, and in 1890, their inexperience lost them the first Army-Navy Game. Captain Michie was killed in Cuba during the Spanish-American War. (Courtesy of Roddy MacLeod.)

ARMY MULES WITH RIDERS. Sixteen mules have been used over the past 100 years, with Raider currently manning the post. At the 1899 Army-Navy Game, the navy brought a goat as a mascot. Army quickly looked for their own mascot. Legendary for their stoutness, army mules were an obvious choice. A specially selected group of cadets ride the army mules, USMA's esteemed mascots, during home football games.

ARMY MULES. A letter *A* is shaved into the hair of each animal's hindquarter and bleached to "Army Gold." One unlucky cadet is assigned the job as "pooper scooper." The current army mule mascots, Raider, Ranger II (also known as George), and General Scott (also known as Scotty), live at the vet clinic behind the craft shop.

MICHIE STADIUM, LUSK RESERVOIR. Michie Stadium overlooks Lusk Reservoir. At the beginning of Beast Barracks, cadets are expected to learn their "knowledge" or lore (commonly referred to as Plebe poop). One question that an upperclassman may demand of a plebe is "How many gallons in Lusk Reservoir?" To which the plebe replies "92.2 million gallons, sir, when the water is flowing over the spillway."

CANNONS AT FOOTBALL GAME. The "cannon crew" discharges cannon fire for every point scored against opponents. The current crew stands ready at Lusk Reservoir east of the stadium eager and ready with a battery of five cannons. The cadets manning the cannon wear ACUs (Army combat uniform) rather than the dress uniform required at the games.

ARVIN GYMNASIUM. Built in 1911 and recently renovated, the Arvin gymnasium houses the Department of Physical Education. An active-duty colonel serving as department head holds the impressive title "Master of the Sword." While many universities are eliminating a physical education requirement, cadets take 168 hours in physical education over four years.

GYMNASIUM—U. S. MILITARY ACADEMY, WEST POINT, N. Y.   20

FRONT FACADE, ARVIN GYMNASIUM. The gymnasium houses two Olympic-sized swimming pools, a wave pool, and a state-of-the-art rock-climbing wall. Historic Hayes Gymnasium, inside Arvin, houses the indoor obstacle course. All must pass the indoor obstacle course each year. It consists of the low crawl, high-step, low vault, shelf mount, traverse high bars, a jump down with dive through tire, balance beam, wall climb, horizontal ladder, vertical rope, and finally, a run.

THAYER MONUMENT, OLD GYMNASIUM. Architect Richard Morris Hunt designed the old gymnasium, constructed in 1891 under Col. Wesley Merritt's superintendence. Pershing Barracks is the only building by Hunt still standing. Sylvanus Thayer's monument, now located on the edge of the plain in front of the commandant's quarters, stood in front of the old gymnasium. Although Thayer defined the academy's mission and formed the basis for the modern academy, he was not popular with cadets. Life under Thayer was difficult. Today, when faced with a particularly punishing week, the cadets may be heard to mutter, "Sure is a Thayer week."

HIGH JUMPING. All cadets participate in team sports. Approximately 30 percent of cadets play intercollegiate athletics; others participate in intramurals and club sports. Over 90 percent of cadets entering West Point have earned at least one varsity letter in high school athletics.

CADETS IN POOL, ARVIN GYMNASIUM. Swimming is taught during plebe year. Plebe swimming, informally known as plebe drowning, is primarily survival swimming. While swimming, cadets wear ACUs and boots while carrying a loaded rucksack and weapon. Marty Maher, the beloved swimming instructor immortalized in the movie *The Long Gray Line*, could not swim.

GOLFING ON TROPHY POINT. Superintendent Douglas MacArthur added golf as an intercollegiate sports team in 1922. All cadets learn a "lifetime" sport—tennis, golf, or skiing. An 18-hole golf course and ski slope provide facilities. Those facilities are now open for public play. The caption on the back of this postcard reads, "The rolling country, overlooking the Hudson River, affords ideal golf links, and during the outdoor life at West Point in the summer, the young men have a considerable interval daily to devote to the healthful Scotch pastime." (Courtesy of Col. [Ret.] Seth Hudgins, USMA 1964.)

FENCING CLASS. History dates fencing from the 1930s. Considered necessary to the development of officers, it was one of the original intercollegiate sports. Currently it holds club status. Boxing is now the primary defensive sport learned by cadets. Taken in the plebe year, the objective in boxing is learning how to react to stressful physical circumstances.

FENCING PRACTICE. Friendly competition is part of most sports at West Point. However, the motto "cooperate and graduate" holds true in athletics as well as academics and militarily. Cadets coach, tutor, and mentor one another throughout their entire four years at the academy.

MILITARY CALISTHENICS. The Army Physical Fitness Test (APFT) includes two minutes of pushups, two minutes of sit-ups, and a two-mile run. The Department of Physical Education administers the test twice per year. If a cadet scores 90 points or better in all three events, he or she is awarded an Army Physical Fitness Badge.

PLATOON CALISTHENICS. Each cadet company determines an individual program of athletics, including company runs, intramural teams, and indoor obstacle course test practice. Cadets deficient in physical fitness receive remedial training from designated upperclassmen. (Courtesy of Col. [Ret.] Seth Hudgins, USMA 1964.)

GYMNASTICS, ARVIN GYMNASIUM. All cadets take gymnastics, called battle movement, during plebe year. Cadets practice rope climbing, tumbling, vaulting, and muscular endurance. (Courtesy of Col. [Ret.] Seth Hudgins, USMA 1964.)

TENNIS. A new tennis facility, the Lichtenberg Tennis Center, opened in 1999. The seven indoor courts feature a hard court surface and an area for viewing matches. Alumni Herb (USMA 1955) and Alan (USMA 1951) Lichtenberg together with the class of 1955 generously donated the funds for the state-of-the-art facility.

POLO. Some of the best polo ponies in the country were at West Point. Horsemanship is once again returning to military training due to conflict in countries such as Afghanistan, where horses are stilled used for transportation in difficult terrain.

Six

THE GLOOM PERIOD
WEATHERING WEST POINT WINTER

CHRISTMAS POSTCARD. Cadets look forward to the holiday dinner for weeks. Plebes begin searching for decorations to fulfill their assignment to decorate tables and have been known to cut live trees from the woods around West Point and drag them into the mess hall. Typically the decorating turns into an informal competition, and lights are strung, costumes worn, and an overall festive evening reigns supreme. The mess hall cooks prepare a traditional turkey dinner with all the trimmings. The evening is finished with cigars (again, provided by the plebes) smoked on the apron in front of Washington Hall. (Courtesy of Col. [Ret.] Seth Hudgins, USMA 1964.)

WINTER VIEW, TAYLOR HALL. After the snows begin to fall, West Point takes on yet another magical quality. Icicles form on the gray stone, snow gathers on the gargoyles, and a quiet hush blankets the post. But then, the snowplows take action and army engineers bring the academy back to life. There are no snow days for cadets, and class is always in session. (Courtesy of Col. [Ret.] Seth Hudgins, USMA 1964.)

WINTER VIEW, FORT PUTNAM. Cadets are issued winter uniforms long before the temperature begins to drop. The cadet long overcoat, worn by the cadet on this postcard, was adopted by superintendent Sylvanus Thayer in 1828. Cadets are also issued leather gloves and a muffler. Female cadets may wear high leather boots with the overcoat. (Courtesy of Col. [Ret.] Seth Hudgins, USMA 1964.)

WINTER VIEW, CENTRAL AREA. Around February, West Point enters a bit of a winter funk commonly referred to as "the gloom period." The short days coupled by weeks of gray skies and the seemingly endless weeks until spring contribute to, arguably, the most difficult time of the year. Victor Constant Ski Slope, located close to Washington Gate, offers a respite for cadets in search of some winter fun. The facility offers snowboarding and skiing with experienced cadets teaching classes. (Courtesy of Col. [Ret.] Seth Hudgins, USMA 1964.)

SNOW AT WEST POINT. Heat is provided by a steam line that runs from the hydroelectric plant in a circuitous route through many of the older buildings on post. Stories of escape routes and secret passages abound but are not confirmed. The valves are opened no earlier than October.

Seven

MUSEUMS
AND MONUMENTS
REMEMBERING THE PAST

THAYER MONUMENT. Sylvanus Thayer, USMA 1808, is buried under a beautiful weeping beech tree in the West Point Cemetery. The Thayer Hotel, Thayer Road, and Thayer Hall are named in honor of the man who is regarded as the man who formed the modern academy. To honor his achievement, West Point established the Thayer Award, "presented to an outstanding citizen whose service and accomplishments in the national interest exemplify the military academy motto, 'Duty, Honor, Country.'" Recipients of the award have included Bob Hope, Billy Graham, Henry Kissinger, Sandra Day O'Connor, and Tom Brokaw.

PATTON'S MONUMENT. Gen. George S. Patton Jr., USMA 1909, became World War II's famous 3rd Army Commander. Patton was deficient in mathematics and took five years to graduate from West Point. When asked why he had difficulty he often responded, "The whole time I was at West Point, I couldn't find the library." His wife, Beatrice, asked that his monument at West Point be placed in front of the library. (Courtesy of Col. [Ret.] Seth Hudgins, USMA 1964.)

DADE MONUMENT. In this view, the Dade Monument is located near Fort Clinton. Erected in memory of Maj. Francis L. Dade and his command of 107 men who were killed by the Seminole Indians in 1835, its current location is just west of the entrance to the West Point Cemetery. The monument has spent some time at the Dade Battlefield in Dade County, Florida.

FRENCH MONUMENT. The L'École Polytechnique Monument, commonly referred to as the French Monument, was a gift from that institution. New cadets memorize the inconsistencies in the statue as part of their plebe knowledge: the saber is curved, the scabbard is straight; the wind blows the flag in one direction, the coat tails in another; the cannon balls are larger than the bore of the cannon; and a button is unbuttoned. It now stands in front of the old First Division barracks located in Central Area.

Battle Monument, U. S. Military Academy, West Point, N. Y.

BATTLE MONUMENT. Dedicated to the soldiers and officers of the regular Union army, Battle Monument serves as the centerpiece to Trophy Point, West Point's outdoor museum. The names of 2,230 killed in the Civil War are inscribed. Civil War cannons surround the base.

BATTLE MONUMENT, RIVERVIEW. Designed by Stanford White, the shaft of Battle Monument is the largest piece of turned granite in the northern hemisphere. Built as a personal tribute by their "surviving brothers," a large number of officers and soldiers of the U.S. Army donated six percent of their salaries for years to pay for the monument.

EDGE OF BATTLE MONUMENT. Although the monument only memorializes the Union dead, 294 West Point graduates served in the Confederate army during the Civil War. Of the 60 major battles in that war, 55 had a West Pointer leading on both sides of the battle. The remaining five had a West Pointer leading on one side or the other.

FIGURE ATOP BATTLE MONUMENT. Frederick MacMonnies sculpted the figure of "Fame" or "Winged Victory," which graces the pinnacle of the monument. The first figure placed atop the monument was deemed inappropriate (her cleavage was exposed, and her legs were bare) and so a second monument was substituted. The artist's model of the original is sometimes on display in the West Point Museum. (Courtesy of Col. [Ret.] Seth Hudgins, USMA 1964.)

Trophy Point, and View of Hudson River, West Point, N. Y.

TROPHY POINT, RIVER. The view from Battle Monument is often referred to as "the million dollar view from West Point." The United States Military Band holds outdoor concerts on Trophy Point during the summer months. The July 4th concert provides the first break new cadets get from summer training. A new cadet in training, one from each state, carries his state flag across the stage.

Trophy Point, showing the Hudson, West Point, N. Y.

CANNONS, TROPHY POINT. The Mexican War contributed 104 cannons and mortars to the collection at West Point. Each is marked with the name and date of the battle. The cannons are now arranged chronologically, and the full history of each gun can be read in the West Point Museum.

CANNON, TROPHY POINT. This postcard pictures the Armstrong Gun, a rifled cannon that guarded Fort Fisher during the Civil War. Captured by Union forces after the fort fell in 1865, it was transported to West Point as a trophy. The gun traveled back to Fort Fisher for an exhibition 135 years later.

MACHINE GUN ROOM. The Department of History maintains historic guns in working order. Periodically the department's officers offer selected cadets an opportunity to fire the historic weapons.

MUSEUM. This postcard shows the museum located in what is now the Thayer Award Room in Taylor Hall. The room now houses a gallery of photographs and biographies of the Thayer Award recipients. Now located at Pershing Center, the West Point Museum is the nation's oldest and largest military museum.

LADYCLIFF ACADEMY. Ladycliff College was an all-female Catholic school that operated on what is now New South Post from 1933 to 1980. After the school closed, West Point purchased the property. The West Point Museum, the visitor's center, temporary housing, and offices are now located on the grounds.

est Point, N.Y. View in West Point Cemetery, U.S. Military Academy.

WEST POINT CEMETERY. A quiet and beautiful location just below Lee Housing area, the West Point Cemetery provides a final resting place for West Point graduates, families, and others associated with the academy and post. The first burials took place in 1817. Many illustrious figures in the nation's history are interred there, including Generals Sylvanus Thayer, Winfield Scott, Robert Anderson, George Custer, Egbert Vielé, Daniel Butterfield, Mickey Marcus, and hundreds more. Others buried in the cemetery include Marty Maher, the Warner sisters, and Margaret Corbin.

GATES, WEST POINT CEMETERY. The wrought iron gates pictured on this postcard were originally located at one of the entrances to West Point. Relocated to the cemetery, they provide a dramatic entrance to the Old Cadet Chapel and cemetery beyond. To the left of the chapel is a memorial to Margaret Corbin. She received a soldier's pension from the U.S. government for her brave service during the Revolutionary War.

ANDERSON FOUNTAIN. Mrs. James Lawton presented the pretty fountain and basin, now located near the caretaker's cottage, in memory of her father, Gen. Robert Anderson, USMA 1825, the defender of Fort Sumter. Anderson, a Kentuckian who supported slavery, remained loyal to the Union. He felt he could help the country avoid Civil War when he took command and withheld firing until Confederate forces bombarded the fort. Sumter fell, and the Civil War began.

Eight

OFFICERS
AND GENTLEMEN
ENTERTAINING FRIENDS

WEST POINT CENTENNIAL. This *c.* 1902 postcard shows Pres. Theodore Roosevelt reviewing the cadets. Ladies and gentleman dressed in their finery lined the parade fields for the centennial celebrations. Graduates and dignitaries hosted parties and receptions, and several commemorative books were published. In 2002, West Point celebrated its bicentennial.

BIEDERMANN PAINTING, AIRSHIPS PASSING WEST POINT. In 1909, an air race took place to commemorate Henry Hudson's discovery of the Hudson River in 1609 and Robert Fulton's trip to Albany in the first steamboat in 1807. At this spectacular event, Wilbur Wright flew his plane with a canoe strapped to the bottom in the event of an emergency water landing. Hundreds of postcards of various scenes along the route were produced. This one, a reproduction of a painting by famous illustrator Louis Biedermann, shows the race passing West Point. The winner of the race received a $10,000 prize.

FLIRTATION WALK, LOOKING SOUTH. A wooded, meandering path curving along the banks of the Hudson River, Flirtation Walk, known as "Flirty," offers a romantic venue for cadets and their dates. Tradition keeps officers and civilians away. The handwritten note on this postcard reads, "I don't see anything to flirt with, do you?"

FLIRTATION WALK AT THE KISSING ROCK. According to tradition, a large rock towering above Flirtation Walk holds the academy's future in abeyance. As a cadet and date pass the rock, they must pause and kiss, otherwise the rock will break away from the side of the mountain and the violent force will draw the walls of West Point into the river. As the walls remain firmly in place, cadets have surely fulfilled the task. No sacrifice is too great.

CADET WITH GUEST ON FLIRTATION WALK. Life at West Point has provided the material for several popular movies, including *Flirtation Walk,* a 1934 musical romance starring Ruby Keeler and Dick Powell. Nominated for best picture, the movie tells the story of the soldier who falls in

love with the general's daughter. The movie was filmed at West Point with the "full cooperation of the army." (Courtesy of Col. [Ret.] Seth Hudgins, USMA 1964.)

STROLLERS, FLIRTATION WALK. Several decades ago (long before the introduction of the computer), cadets would pack picnics and their "green girls" in typewriter cases for a private dinner with a favorite female friend. A green girl refers to an issued green blanket named such by the cadets because "you spend more time in bed with it than anyone else."

PRIVATE MOMENT, FLIRTATION WALK. Many proposals of marriage have been offered and accepted on West Point's lovers' lane. Two percent of cadets marry high school sweethearts and earn membership in the "Two-Percent Club," an honorable distinction earned by patience and commitment. In the early days, a cadet may have offered his girlfriend a "spoony button," a full-dress button. Today's cadets may offer a miniature of a West Point ring—usually reserved for a wife or fiancée.

FLIRTATION WALK ENTRANCE. Prior to the Civil War, Flirtation Walk was known as "Chain Battery Walk" because it led to the battery guarding the great chain. Cadets in search of a tan after a long winter sunbathe on Flirty's "beach." (Courtesy of Roddy MacLeod.)

PICNICKING AT WEST POINT. The scenery and private areas make picnicking at West Point a great way to spend an afternoon. There are picnic grounds at South Dock on the lower level of academy grounds. The river's edge provides a nice vantage point for watching the sailing team or crew team practice on the Hudson River.

VISITORS AT WEST POINT. Significant events in the cadet calendar draw thousands of friends and family to West Point. Plebe Parent Weekend in the fall offers the fourth-class cadets an opportunity to invite guests to demonstrations of activities, a formal dinner in the mess hall, and a formal hop. (Courtesy of Col. [Ret.] Seth Hudgins, USMA 1964.)

VISITORS ON TROPHY POINT. Family and friends fill the post during "Ring Weekend." During the fall semester, Firsties receive their USMA class rings. As part of the tradition, plebes pester the upperclassmen with the following jingle: "Oh my Gawd Sir, what a beautiful ring. What a crass mass of brass and glass. What a bold mold of rolled gold. What a cool jewel you got from your school. See how it sparkles and shines. It must have cost you a fortune. May I touch it, may I touch it please, Sir? Pleeeeeeze." (Courtesy of Col. [Ret.] Seth Hudgins, USMA 1964.)

HOP, CULLUM HALL. Until the construction of Eisenhower Hall, Cullum Memorial Hall provided the backdrop for beautiful hops. Historically young ladies from the surrounding area, including New York City, have eagerly traveled to West Point to dance with the dashing young cadets in their beautiful uniforms. The dance cards for most visitors were always full. According to the 1928 *Bugle Notes*, " 'Cutting in' on young ladies with whom one is acquainted is permitted on encores." (Courtesy of Col. [Ret.] Seth Hudgins, USMA 1964.)

EST POINT. Dancing.

This place is to dead for me — W. S

Copyright by Waldon Fawcett

CADET DANCE CLASS. In 1823, West Point hired a "dancing master" and formal dance training began. One dancing master, Edward Ferrero, was mustered into the army during the Civil War where he received a battlefield commission to brigadier general at Antietam. Enthusiastic cadet Dwight Eisenhower, USMA 1915, received punishment during one dance for "Violation of orders in reference to dancing, having previously been admonished for the same offense." According to Eisenhower, he had been admonished for twirling his partner on the dance floor and later got carried away again and twirled her again, exposing "ankle and maybe even a little knee." The note scribbled on the front of the postcard reads, "This place is to dead for me." Many cadets have thought the same thing.

CADET COLORS AND GUARDS. The American flag and dress parades at West Point take on a special significance. West Point is the oldest continually garrisoned post in the United States. Troops have been stationed here since 1778. The cadets wearing the red sash are seniors. A flag ceremony is held each day at reveille and retreat. A drummer and bugler from the band and military personnel play reveille and retreat, raise or lower the flag, and fire the cannon. On military posts, all personnel, civilian and military, stop and face the flag during the ceremony.

CADET PARADE, REVIEWING PARTY. During his tenure as superintendent, Sylvanus Thayer sought opportunities to introduce the public to the cadets and West Point. Cadets were generally popular wherever they went, and public support for the academy increased after several summer marches arranged by Thayer. The public was also welcomed to West Point to view dress parades.

RETREAT PARADE ON THE PLAIN. The corps presents up to 20 dress parades each year. The beautiful plain with Washington Hall and the Cadet Chapel as backdrop provides a spectacular setting for the academy's young men and women as they march the historic field—the second-most-expensive "lawn" in the country.

98

SUMMER CAMP PARADE. Cadets march with their companies. At present, there are four regiments. Each regiment consists of eight companies. The company staff presents the company at the superintendent's reviewing stand by the command, "Eyes right!" All the rows of cadets closest to the viewing stand shift their gaze to the right and salute. "Eyes right" represents a salute in marching formation.

USMA COLOR GUARD. The color guard now marches with the American flag, the army flag, and the USMA flag. Each company marches with their guidon, identifying their regiment and company. The stiff winds on the parade field often prove challenging for the standard bearers.

CORPS OF CADET COLORS. The USMA crest includes an American bald eagle and a scroll with the motto Duty, Honor, Country and the words and number "West Point, MDCCCII." The helmet of Pallas Athena on a Greek sword displayed on a shield complete the coat of arms. The corps of cadets flag displays the cadet colors, black, gray, and gold. The colors are from the components of gunpowder: charcoal, saltpeter (potassium nitrate), and sulphur. (Courtesy of Col. [Ret.] Seth Hudgins, USMA 1964.)

CADETS MARCHING TO DINNER. Cadets now march in "blended" formation. In the past, formations were arranged by height with the "runts" in front and the "flankers" in the back. On the northeast corner of the parade field there was a depression known as Execution Hollow. During the Revolutionary War, executions took place there.

CADETS AT INSPECTION. Full-dress parades take place before significant events in the academy's calendar, including Acceptance Day, Ring Weekend, graduation, and home football games. The corps may also give a parade in honor of visiting dignitaries. Cadets have marched for several presidents, foreign heads of state, and even visiting navy admirals.

SALUTING THE COLORS. Generally parades are not a favorite activity for cadets. Cadets have been known to pray to Odin, a mythical Norse god, for significant rain, an event that would cancel the parade. Prayers are also made to Odin for cancellation of in-ranks inspections. From time to time, prayers are answered.

VISITORS VIEWING PARADE. Preparing for a full-dress parade requires hours of drilling on the parade field in all kinds of weather. Mastering drill technique is critical and includes learning drill commands, rifle drill, and infinite patience. All windows in the barracks facing the plain must be closed during the parade, and no cadets (those not marching) may be viewed from the windows. (Courtesy of Col. [Ret.] Seth Hudgins, USMA 1964.)

RELIEF OF THE GUARD. Initially West Point cadets dressed in a blue uniform. A shortage of blue dye necessitated the switch to gray uniforms. The uniforms have undergone minor modifications throughout the years, but the gray cloth remains as part of the "Long Gray Line."

CADET REGIMENTAL STAFF. Cadet insignia reflects rank and position. For example, a regimental commander wears six chevrons; a battalion commander wears five chevrons; and a battalion sergeant major wears two chevrons and one arc. Cadets with high academic honors wear a star and a wreath, representing military and physical excellence. (Courtesy of Col. [Ret.] Seth Hudgins, USMA 1964.)

WAITING FOR DRESS PARADE CALL. Sometimes it seems the army's motto should be "hurry up and wait." A large measure of patience is needed to endure the waiting. That waiting begins on Reception Day when the cadets wait for uniform issues, haircuts, medical checks, new glasses, briefing, and the attention of upperclassmen.

SUMMER CAMP INSPECTION. The present version of the full-dress hat, known as a "tarbucket" or shako, was first used in 1962. The modifications throughout the years have been relatively minor and include a nontarnishing chain, a very welcome change. In the event of a windy day, the cadet can hold the chinstrap between his teeth to keep the hat from blowing off. Officers wear plums, and the others wear poms.

CADET ON SENTRY DUTY. When outside, a cadet must always be "covered," wearing a hat. In addition to the tarbucket, each cadet is issued four other styles of hat: gray saucer hat, white saucer hat (the one that's tossed at graduation), garrison cap (the narrow, flat hat typically worn on class days), and the ACU hat. Decades ago, the sentry "houses," as pictured on this postcard, were found at intervals around post. One has been preserved in the garden of Quarters 100.

CADETS READY FOR DRESS PARADE. The white belt on the dress uniform is a standard cartridge belt. When former West Point cadet Edgar Allen Poe was in attendance a command was issued: "All cadets assemble for parade in white cross belts." The story purports that Poe arrived for parade in belts—but naked otherwise. He was dismissed.

USMA BAND. The USMA Band traces its beginnings to the Revolutionary War era. In 1827, the USMA Band, the first army band, organized. Cadets were required to contribute 25¢ each month for the support of the musicians. (Courtesy of Col. [Ret.] Seth Hudgins, USMA 1964.)

CONCERT BAND. The current band consists of four parts: a concert band, the Hellcats (drums and bugles), a jazz band, and the support staff. Recruited from the finest music schools in the United States and auditioned in a very competitive process, band members are soldiers and musicians. Once selected, the band member attends basic training like every other soldier. Primarily noncommissioned officers, band members may spend an entire military career at West Point. (Courtesy of Col. [Ret.] Seth Hudgins, USMA 1964.)

BAND IN MARCHING FORMATION. The band marches with the corps during all parades, and drummers and buglers keep marching tempo for formations. Drummers and buglers also open the day at reveille and close the day with retreat, providing an audible structure to cadet life. (Courtesy of Col. [Ret.] Seth Hudgins, USMA 1964.)

OUTDOOR CONCERT. As part of its duties, the band performs concerts throughout the year. The outdoor performances at Trophy Point are especially anticipated. The public is welcomed to West Point to picnic and enjoy a beautiful evening listening to one of the finest bands in the world. The July 4th concert always includes Tchaikovsky's "1812 Overture" with live cannon fire and fireworks.

BAND BARRACKS, WEST POINT, N.Y.

BAND BARRACKS. Constructed in the 1870s, the historic band barracks was razed in 1970 to make way for Eisenhower Hall. Housing for band personnel and families is now located next to Keller Army Hospital. Many band members spend an entire military career at West Point.

CADET GLEE CLUB. In some form or another, cadets have always enjoyed singing. In the early days, boisterous drinking songs filled Benny Havens (the local tavern frequented by cadets), and spirit songs have long been a part of the academy. In 1903, the official USMA Glee Club formed and gave its first performance in March of that year. Eighty-eight cadets currently sing in the mixed choir that travels throughout the world and offers up to 50 concerts each year. The performance of the alma mater is especially poignant.

Nine

THREE MILLION TOURISTS A YEAR
VISITING WEST POINT

CADET AT GUARD DUTY. This postcard is captioned "Cadet Challenging, 'Who Comes There?'" The main answer to that demand would be the great American public. Traveling by boat, train, and automobile, millions of visitors are welcomed by West Point throughout the year. Football season and graduation record the highest number of people entering the gates.

GARRISON FERRY. Prior to the building of bridges across the river, Hudson River ferries carried passengers and cars back and forth across the river. Tickets on the *Highlander* cost $1.50 for a car and driver, and single passengers paid 25¢. West Point boats carry cadets across the river to the Garrison train station. (Courtesy of John and June Gunza.)

DAY LINE STEAMERS. A guide to West Point, dated 1900, gives the following information: "The regular steamboat lines landing here are: The Hudson River Day Line, and the Central Hudson passenger and freight line." In the early 19th century, steamboats became a fashionable way to travel the Hudson to view the grandeur and beauty of the river. Of course, USMA was a popular destination.

STEAMER WASHINGTON IRVING PASSING WEST POINT, HUDSON RIVER, N. Y.

THE WASHINGTON IRVING. The river has served military and commercial purposes since before the Revolution. After the invention of the steamboat by Robert Fulton in 1807, leisure travel on the Hudson grew in popularity. By 1850, approximately 150 steamboats traveled the Hudson River, carrying thousands of passengers to cities, amusement parks, and historic sites.

HUDSON RIVER DAY LINE. Many postcards, such as this one, were sold aboard the steamboats. The caption on the back reads, "The Hudson River, the great Tourist Throughfare of America, is unsurpassed in historic interest, beauty, and charm. The Palatial Steamers Hendrick Hudson, Robert Fulton and Albany of the Day Line are the finest, fastest, cleanest and best manned river steamers in the world, and offer the ideal way to view the river."

THE MARY POWELL. The great steamboat *Mary Powell* brought George Armstrong Custer's body from Poughkeepsie to West Point to be buried. The funeral party was beyond the capacity for the *Mary Powell*, and as it docked, it took on water. Luckily disaster was averted. Custer was originally buried at Little Big Horn, but his wife, Elizabeth Bacon, insisted that her husband's remains be exhumed and brought to West Point—with full honors. A body was recovered, although some question to its identity remains. His original monument featured a statue of Custer. Elizabeth did not like the likeness and had it removed.

ALBANY DAY BOAT NEW YORK AT LANDING, WEST POINT, N. Y.

ALBANY DAY BOAT. With the opening of the railroads and roads, river travel slowed somewhat, although cruises on the Hudson River are still popular. Several cruise ship companies arrange tours that stop at West Point. Some are overnight cruises that begin in New York City and end in Albany—tracing Henry Hudson's route.

STORM KING BYPASS. Route 9W forms the Storm King Bypass. Leading from West Point to Cornwall-on-Hudson, the scenic highway offers several parking areas for sightseers to stop and enjoy a bird's-eye view of the academy and the Highlands. Hiking on the mountain is also an attraction in the area.

ROAD FROM HIGHLAND FALLS. Highland Falls, known originally as Buttermilk Falls, adjoins West Point at Thayer Gate. The stores, restaurants, and accommodations provide services for visitors, cadets, and residents of the academy. Highland Falls and West Point's histories intertwine, and their symbiotic relationship continues today.

OLD TRAIN STATION. In the not-so-distant past, railroad travel was the primary means for reaching West Point. The West Shore Railroad opened in 1883. To make way for the tracks, the railroad constructed a tunnel that stretches below the post for three-fifths of a mile. The old depot was Victorian and was replaced in 1924.

NEW TRAIN STATION. The "new" train station, now known as the Cadet Activity Club, provided a modern facility for train travelers. The Gothic-style architecture and lavish interior belie its small size. Restored by the USMA class of 1947, it accommodates up to 35 people and includes a fully equipped kitchen.

WEST POINT HOTEL. The West Point Hotel, built in 1829 and demolished in the early 1930s, stood on the eastern point of the plain. Cadet Douglas MacArthur's mother, "Pinkie," occupied one of the rooms for the duration of her son's tenure at the academy. Purportedly she left "boodle" (cadet slang for snacks) for him in cannons on Trophy Point and watched for his lights to extinguish in his barracks room.

THAYER HOTEL. Located immediately inside Thayer Gate, the Thayer Hotel was built to accommodate the growing number of visitors to the academy. Completed in 1926, Presidents Dwight D. Eisenhower, John F. Kennedy, Richard Nixon, Gerald Ford, and George H. W. Bush have stayed as guests in the presidential suite. Acquired by a group of graduates in 1999, an ambitious renovation restored the hotel to its former grandeur. A new wing doubled its size. A civilian corporation leases and operates the hotel.

RIVERSIDE, THAYER HOTEL. The hotel remains a popular site for weddings, wedding receptions, and conferences. The hotel schedules special entertainment throughout the year. In the summer months, the hotel offers outdoor dining on the terrace, where guests enjoy spectacular views of the Hudson River and Constitution Island. Their Web site provides dates and information.

The Lobby
The Thayer-West Point
West Point, N. Y.

LOBBY, THAYER HOTEL. A grand oak door opens onto the marble floors of the lobby. Circular candle chandeliers hang above comfortable seating areas. An enormous fireplace provides the centerpiece. During the holiday season, the hotel hosts a reception after the tree-lighting ceremony as a gift to the community. Unfailingly generous in its support of West Point, the hotel is an integral part of life at the academy. (Courtesy of John and June Gunza.)

DINING ROOM, THAYER HOTEL. Sunday brunch at the Thayer Hotel is a Hudson Valley tradition. The kitchen is staffed by Culinary Institute of America graduates and provides gracious dining for West Point visitors. A daily lunch buffet is open for casual dining. (Courtesy of John and June Gunza.)

BALLROOM, THAYER HOTEL. The ballroom at the Thayer Hotel can accommodate a large wedding reception. Weddings at West Point are typically military—complete with dress blues and a saber arch. Friends of the bride and/or groom form an arch with sabers, and the bride and groom exit the ceremony under the arch. A military tradition allows one of the saber bearers to bring his saber down and swat the bride on the bottom as she passes—an unofficial welcome to army life. The tradition is a bit outdated but colorful nonetheless. (Courtesy of John and June Gunza.)

MEMORIAL HALL BALLROOM. Many young women met their future husbands while visiting West Point. Cadets often sent invitations to their favorite girls. The note on this postcard postmarked 1932 reads, "Dear Maria Elena, I've had a perfectly marvelous time. The dance last nite was wonderful, and Harry is swell! The picture on this card is where the dance was. It was to be outside, and everything was decorated beautifully, but it rained. We're going home a 4 o'clock this afternoon. I'd like to stay longer. Wish you could come here some time. You'd like it. Love, Grace."

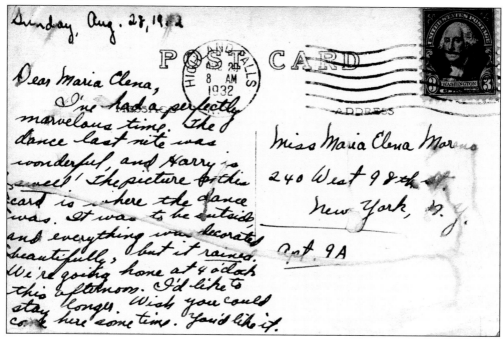

ANDERSON GUN TROPHY POINT. Cadets used postcards to write notes home to anxious families. The note on this card, postmarked 1932, reads, "Hello Everyone, No one knows what this place is like until after he enters. We have just started academics, and it is hard to get used to the way they teach. Good luck to the whole family. Dean." (Courtesy of Col. [Ret.] Seth Hudgins, USMA 1964.)

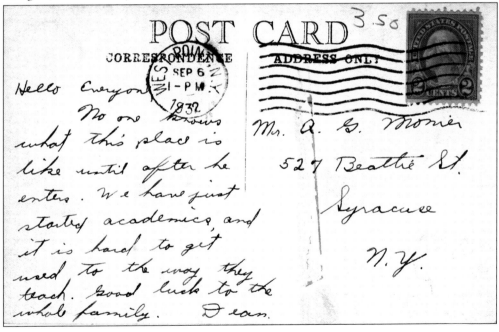

BATTALION PASSING IN REVIEW. Parades were always popular with visitors. The cadets make it appear easy, but countless hours contribute to the perfect formations. Children often mimic the marching for days after a visit. The note on this card, postmarked 1908, states, "Dear George, This is how the cadets marched yesterday. We took Charles up with us and he was very much interested in seeing the cadets march and when we got home he was showing us how to march. Love from Clementine."

STANDING INSPECTION AT CADET CAMP. This postcard sent from an address in Highland Falls attempts to entice someone to visit by promises of visits to West Point. When assigned to West Point or living in the area, houseguests enjoy seeing the academy and cadets. "How would you like to become one of these boys? If you come down we will see these fellows. Mama and Papa said they would very much like you to visit us. Be sure and let me know at once whether you are coming and if you are, what day. We will have a great time. Esther."

OLD LIBRARY. Although the sender of the postcard, postmarked 1910, seems to have enjoyed the river trip, many other riverboat passengers found themselves with motion sickness. This card reads, "Trip up Hudson was one dream [crossed out 'one dream' and 'very fine' penciled in]. Went thru several buildings and saw the finest dress-parade ever. Some [crossed out and 'There are' penciled in] classy cadets up here. Meta ought to be along. Lovingly Elsa."

MEMORIAL HALL. This postcard, addressed to a "Miss," was probably written by a smitten cadet to a young lady after a hop. Note the horse-drawn carriage that has been drawn in by the sender. He writes in tiny script, " 'After the Ball is Over' What becomes of Grover? Have you recovered from the effects of the dances with the elephant?"

VISITORS REVIEWING DRESS PARADE. This postcard shows visitors watching the parade from chairs set up on the plain. Bleachers now offer ample seating. The writer of this postcard wrote on the front of the card, "Some day you will go to West Point. I hope." The back of the card reads, "Hello Bob, How is everything down South, we had a 96 temp for the last few days, it is cool again, and plenty of rain, Everything is about the same here, quiet as usual. I am in a hell of a mess at the Point we can't cut the lawns on account of the gasoline ban. Hoping to see you soon try and save some of your money. Loving Pop."

Steamer Hendrick Hudson, passing through the Highlands, Hudson River, N. Y.

STEAMSHIPS ON HUDSON RIVER. Parents enjoy visiting their cadets, and all of a sudden those sullen teenagers are transformed. The note on this postcard, postmarked 1915, reads "It is like heaven. Our dear Yearling Corporal is an Apollo. He seems very happy although he did not make the middle of the class. He expects betters luck next year when he has no history . . . His friends are fine. Mostly Army boys and I like them as much as ——. C.K.M."

West Point and the Hudson River

THAYER ROAD. Four entrances lead to West Point. The main entrance through Highland Falls, Thayer Gate, passes the Thayer Hotel and continues down Thayer Road and brings visitors to the cadet areas and Trophy Point. Stony Lonesome Gate, convenient to the parking lots at Michie Stadium, is also open to visitors for special events. Several parking lots on Stony Lonesome Road are reserved for cadet cars—only Firsties may keep a car at West Point.

211864

CADETS OFF DUTY. USMA is the only service academy that still makes its own uniforms. A factory, located on the lower level of West Point, employs several dozen seamstresses, cutters, and tailors. At one point, most of the tailors were Italian professionals. Cadets often make the

CADETS OFF DUTY

trek down to the factory for fittings. Even when they have a little leisure time, plebes must dress in uniform outside the barracks.

WORLD WAR I SOUVENIR CARD. Soldiers far from home have always sent postcards assuring loved ones that all is well and "I'll be home soon." Letters from home provide tremendous comfort and a bit of distraction for soldiers stationed away from loved ones. Throughout history, the ones left at home anxiously want for the mail carrier to bring news. Although technology has altered the way most people communicate, nothing replaces the experience of real mail. So when visiting somewhere, choose a postcard and send it to a soldier.

BIBLIOGRAPHY

Cowley, Robert and Thomas Guinzburg, eds. *West Point: Two Centuries of Honor and Tradition.* New York: Time Warner, 2002.

Crackel, Theodore J. *West Point: A Bicentennial History.* Lawrence, KS: University Press of Kansas, 2002.

————. *The Illustrated History of West Point.* New York: Harry N. Abrams, A Time Mirror Company, 1991.

Dineen, Joseph E. *The Illustrated Sports at the United States Military Academy.* Norfolk, VA: The Donning Company, 1988.

Engeman, Jack. *West Point: The Life of a Cadet.* New York: Lothrop, Lee and Shepard Company, Inc., 1956.

Foley, James E., John D. Hard, and Ernie Webb. *West Point Sketch Book: USMA Bicentennial Edition.* Bloomington, IN: Authorhouse, 2004.

Grant, John, James Lynch, and Ronald Bailey. *West Point: The First 200 Years.* Guilford, CT: The Globe Pequot Press, 2002.

Lankevich, George J. *River of Dreams: The Hudson Valley in Historic Postcards.* New York: Fordham University Press, 2006.

Miller, Rod. *The Campus Guide: West Point U.S. Military Academy.* New York: Princeton Architectural Press, 2002.

Poughkeepsie Journal. *West Point: Legend on the Hudson.* Poughkeepsie, NY: Poughkeepsie Journal, 2003.

Simpson, Jeffrey. *Officers and Gentleman: Historic West Point in Photographs.* Tarrytown, NY: Sleepy Hollow Press, 1982.

DISCOVER THOUSANDS OF LOCAL HISTORY BOOKS FEATURING MILLIONS OF VINTAGE IMAGES

Arcadia Publishing, the leading local history publisher in the United States, is committed to making history accessible and meaningful through publishing books that celebrate and preserve the heritage of America's people and places.

Find more books like this at
www.arcadiapublishing.com

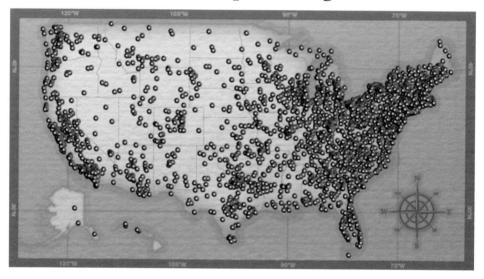

Search for your hometown history, your old stomping grounds, and even your favorite sports team.